AF317025

THE WAR TO WEALTH

The War to Wealth

How a Marine Learned to Build Wealth, Discipline, and a Life Without Limits Through Real Estate

Austin Hancock

Published by Game Changer Publishing

Paperback ISBN: 979-8-90158-204-6
Hardcover ISBN: 979-8-90158-111-7
Digital ISBN: 979-8-90158-112-4

www.GameChangerPublishing.com

DEDICATION

I dedicated this book to my wife, Alysha. My "ride or die." The biggest decision impacting your success is the person you spend your life with... the person closest to you. Success is not merely money alone but peace when the world is loud, when business is hard, when doubt creeps in, and when everything is thriving or surviving. Who you share this with matters. Thank you. You are an amazing mother to our two daughters and my soulmate.

I also want to thank my parents, Mike and Tamra Hancock, for setting the example of a strong foundation at home. I knew that whether I succeeded or failed, I had a place where people loved and supported me regardless.

READ THIS FIRST

If you are ready to take the next steps, want guidance to avoid mistakes, are committed, and are serious about living your life by design, scan the QR code below, and let's have a conversation.

Scan the QR Code Here:

THE
WAR
TO
WEALTH

How a Marine Learned to Build Wealth, Discipline,
and a Life Without Limits Through Real Estate

AUSTIN HANCOCK

FOREWORD

When you command a Marine infantry battalion in combat, you see a lot of young men in a very short period of time. Over a thousand. They come through your unit at eighteen, nineteen, twenty years old, and most of them are trying to figure out who they are while simultaneously, earnestly learning the skills and tactics they need to succeed in combat. You remember the ones who stood out. Austin Hancock was one of those Marines.

I was the battalion commander when Austin deployed with us to Iraq in 2007 and 2008. Austin was assigned as part of a small group of Marines who were part of my daily patrol. What I remember about him is what I remember about a lot of the best young Marines I served with: he was tough, he was fit, and he trained and took correction in a way a warrior does when the respect of their peers matters. What made Austin stand out was his obvious determination to get better each day by doing the little things right.

Every single day, he took the coaching and correction of the demanding NCOs and staff NCOs around him. Anyone who has spent time in an infantry battalion knows that is no small thing. Those men set a standard that will build Marines who are determined to grow, and expose those who are not.

Austin was serious. You could see it. He wasn't the most polished Marine in the battalion, and I'm sure he'd be the first to tell you that. But he showed up every day with the kind of commitment that is not self-promoting or spectacular in the moment. Over time, however, it becomes remarkable.

What I didn't know then, and what I learned reading this book, was just how much Austin had been carrying with him when he showed up to our battalion. Two felonies and two misdemeanors by the age of seventeen. A judge who gave him a choice between juvenile detention and the Marine Corps. A young man who had every reason to go sideways and instead chose the hardest path available to him. When I think about that now, knowing what I knew of him as a young Marine grinding it out every day under the watchful eyes of some very demanding leaders, it places what I observed of him in context. He wasn't just trying to be a good Marine. He was trying to become a different man.

This book is the story of what happened after he succeeded at that. The path Austin describes after leaving the Corps is one that will be familiar to a lot of veterans. The restlessness. The sense that the civilian world doesn't quite fit anymore. The search for something that demands as much of you as combat did. Austin found that in entrepreneurship, first in construction and then in real estate. The candid story he tells is not a straight line. It is full of mistakes, near-bankruptcy, sleepless nights, and the kind of gut-check moments that remind you of what it felt like to be nineteen years old signing your will before a deployment.

What I admire about Austin's story, and what I think makes this book worth reading, is that he doesn't pretend any of it was easy. He doesn't skip over the parts where he was arrogant, or ignorant, or flat-out wrong. He tells you about writing a $65,000 check at a closing table just to get out from under a house that was drowning him. He tells you about moving his young family into a rental after selling the dream home he'd built with his own hands. He tells you about the fear and the doubt and the nights on the treadmill at three in the morning trying to figure out how to save his business and his family. And he is candid about the fact that he didn't do it alone—his wife stood beside him through every pivot and setback, eventually creating the trajectory for the real estate side of their business almost entirely by herself.

That is the Austin Hancock I recognize. Not the multi-millionaire sitting in a four- million-dollar house in San Diego, though I am incredibly proud that he got there. The Austin I recognize is the one who kept showing up. The one who kept grinding. The one who accepted every blow without breaking and simply woke up the next day believing that he could endure, evolve and succeed.

It's no surprise to me that Austin eventually figured it out. I watched him do it for over a year nearly twenty years ago, surrounded by Marines who demanded his best every day, and I see now that he never stopped doing it after he took off the uniform. He accepted his mistakes, owned them completely, educated himself, pivoted when he needed to, and built something remarkable. All while holding his young family together. That is the mark of a resilient leader who willingly bears the responsibility for his family, business and critical relationships. It is the mark of the man Austin has become.

If you are a veteran trying to find your footing in the civilian world, read this book. If you are a young person who has made mistakes and thinks the road is closed, read this book. If you are anyone who has ever wondered whether the discipline and grit you learned the hard way can translate into something bigger—not just wealth, but a life built around the people who matter most—read this book. Austin Hancock is living proof that it can.

Semper Fidelis,

David Bellon
Lieutenant General, USMC (Ret.)

TABLE OF CONTENTS

INTRODUCTION

My name is Austin Hancock. I was once a troubled teenager, a former Marine infantryman, and a construction worker. Now I'm an entrepreneur and, ultimately, an outsider.

I never wanted to fit into a mold or settle for a life that didn't align with my desires. Creating my version of success has always been my top priority, and I believe in bringing along the people I love on this journey. Throughout this book, I'll share my story, the lessons I've learned, and insights you can apply to your life.

I hope that as you read this book, you feel inspired to take action and create the life you truly deserve for yourself and your family. Today, I'm a multimillionaire, owning millions in real estate and living my dream every single day. I'm able to work with people I choose and live where and how I want.

My aim is to inspire others to realize that they can achieve their dreams as well.

CHAPTER 1

Facing two felonies and two misdemeanors at the age of seventeen was not what my parents envisioned for me when I was growing up. However, I had made my decision, and now I had to reap what I had sown.

Growing up in Oklahoma, I had a great life. My parents did everything they could to keep me out of trouble. We went to church on Sundays, played baseball, and participated in various sports. Essentially, they did all the things that good parents do. They were involved in my life, stayed married, and still are. We were a picture-perfect middle-class family in the Midwest.

My father, who graduated from college with an engineering degree, was a smart man. He never got in trouble, didn't drink, and was truly a good example for me. My mom took on the responsibility of raising us while my dad worked. She was always there to help us and drive us around, and she allowed us the freedom to play outside, ride our bikes to friends' houses, and have sleepovers. It was the 1990s, before the internet really took off, and we didn't realize how good life was.

The worst of our troubles back then was buying the wrong CD, maybe something by Blink-182, learning a few bad words, or getting into some light mischief with friends, like throwing rocks or having fistfights at the park. It was a sheltered version of America.

However, as I grew older and went through puberty, I began to test the boundaries of my parents' authority and the societal rules I was raised with. While the morals and values instilled in me remained strong, I found it hard to take advice from my parents, as I perceived their lack of experience at the time. I grew up watching combat movies featuring action heroes like Arnold Schwarzenegger and Sylvester Stallone, who seemed to live life to the fullest.

Even before I could drive, I started creating my own ghillie suits, playing paintball, and pretending sticks were guns. My freshman year began in 2001, the year of the World Trade Center attacks, and long before I turned seventeen, I had already decided I wanted to enlist in the military.

Initially, my parents had no issue with my wish to join, but they became concerned when they realized that I would almost certainly be going to war. I think that bothered them more than anything else. There was a period between my freshman and senior years of high school when they likely hoped I would change my mind. Ultimately, things turned out in my favor.

Despite growing up with good parents and having their guidance, like most young men, I wanted to forge my own path and test my limits physically, mentally, and emotionally. My friend groups began to change throughout high school, especially after I stopped wrestling, a sport I had participated in for nine years.

My dad, being an athlete, had been offered a wrestling & baseball scholarship to college when he was young and was a strong advocate for the sports. He got me involved in wrestling when I was just six years old, which made me competitive. In high school, I also participated in cross-country and track, but ultimately, I wanted to build muscle, and in my senior year, I quit all sports and started going to the gym to lift weights and get bigger. Changing my focus led me to more free time outside of the gym with different friend groups, which nudged me toward testing the limits of alcohol and engaging in increasingly reckless behavior.

I went from being a kid innocently riding bikes and jumping over my friends via dirt jumps to a reckless teen attending field parties, which almost always ended in fistfights or trouble. Thankfully, I never fell into the trap of drug use, but I definitely pushed the boundaries with alcohol, often staying out late and lying to my parents. By the time I was seventeen, I had two pending felonies and two misdemeanors. My rebellious behavior was catching up to me.

The situation I found myself in was a result of the decisions I had made, and I know now that many young men felt the same way, not knowing how to channel their energy positively. Often, this energy gets bottled up or expressed through negative actions. However, some wise young men choose to express it in constructive ways. My goal was to join the military, but my pending criminal record threatened that dream.

One bad decision I made was changing my friend groups. I moved away from my innocent adolescent friends, the ones I used to ride bikes and play with, and started hanging out with a more aggressive crowd. I left behind the nerdier guys and began spending time with my sports teammates and with some of the guys I met in auto body and collision classes while working on cars.

I was obsessed with car culture. At fifteen, I would ride my bike to the local gas station and buy *Autotrader* magazines in search of the perfect truck. I was thrilled to have my own vehicle. I felt very fortunate to have it, and I spent all my savings customizing it. However, when I got into trouble, I had no choice but to sell the truck to cover the deposit for an attorney.

After I received those charges, rumors at school spread, claiming I had either killed or severely injured someone, which made the situation seem much worse than it was. The charges

I faced included attempted assault with a deadly weapon, first-degree burglary, and vandalism, with the two misdemeanors also being related to vandalism.

One night, I found myself at a party where we were outside, but we were quickly ushered inside because the cops were patrolling the neighborhood. This was pretty normal for the college area where I was hanging out, even though I was only seventeen. Once inside the house, I realized I didn't know the owner. It was a big party, filled with lots of people.

A few of my friends were there because we had all been shuffled in together. Attending parties like this was a regular occurrence for us on weekends and even on some weeknights. I often lied to my parents, telling them I was doing something else or that I would be staying at a friend's house. In reality, I had no idea where I would crash or who I would be with.

Sometimes, I would have the friends my parents thought I was with drop me off at these parties, only to hang out with other buddies I knew from auto body and collision classes. In this particular situation, my life changed in an instant.

At the party, a guy approached me. He claimed to be the homeowner or the person leasing the property, a college student around twenty-one years old. He asked me, "Did you talk to my sister?"

"I've talked to a lot of people at this party," I replied. I pride myself on my morals and values, and I never push boundaries with anyone. However, I didn't understand what he was getting at.

He invited me outside to talk, saying, "I think you did." It was loud in the house, so I agreed. Before we did, I waved to one of my friends. He came over, and I said to him, "Hey, I want you to watch my back. I don't know what's going on with this guy."

Once outside, the guy asked me again if I had talked to his sister, and before I could respond, he punched me in the face. My instincts kicked in as a wrestler, and I took him down with a double-leg takedown.

We ended up on the ground, fighting. Fistfights weren't new to me at that point in my life; just a few months prior, I had been involved in a larger altercation that had brought my father into the mix, as the fight had escalated in front of my parents' house after our opponents had followed us home.

My parents were already concerned about the path I was taking, and as this situation unfolded, I knew they would be worried even more. I continued to fight with the guy, and my friend started fighting with one of the guy's friends. So, it became two against two.

No weapons, just fighting. After they jumped us, we scrapped and finally got away by jumping the front fence, walking off with a black eye and a few bruises that fueled a desire for vengeance.

We were very angry, and anger can completely blind you, leading you to make decisions that can alter your life forever.

We jumped the fence and got into the unlocked truck of another friend of ours. I grabbed a tire iron, and my buddy grabbed another tool for changing tires. Then we headed to the front door. One of the people attending the party opened the door and said, "Hey, man, I don't know what your problem is, but it's over."

I distinctly remember smacking him across the arm with the tire iron. I don't know how badly I injured him, but he stumbled back and slammed the door on us, refusing to let us back in.

In our anger, we started smashing the windows in the front of the house and vandalizing the vehicles in the driveway, which we assumed belonged to the people renting the house. We were determined to take revenge. We didn't understand why we had been attacked, and we wanted to escalate things.

Next, we decided to rally the troops and bring a few more of our friends. We jumped back into the unlocked truck, drove away in it, and picked up four or five of our friends who were at IHOP, likely drunk and getting some late-night food.

I'll never forget walking down the street toward that house after parking down the street. The guys we brought had graduated the year before us, so they were a bit older. One of them kicked in the front door, and the guy who had jumped me was right there.

My friend asked, "Is this the guy who jumped you?"

"Yeah," I said, and the moment I entered the premises, I caught a burglary charge. I didn't steal anything, but I entered without being welcomed.

I struck the guy who had attacked me over the head with the tire iron. Almost immediately, blood gushed from his wound because, as you may know, head injuries tend to bleed excessively and quickly. That's when the reality of my actions hit me. All my anger and blind pursuit of revenge stopped abruptly as I realized the gravity of what I had done.

He didn't collapse right away. Instead, he stumbled around and tried to grab me, reminiscent of our earlier confrontation. I quickly handed off the tire iron and wrestled him back to the ground. After pushing him down, I got off him. I had taken off my shirt and was now covered in his blood. As I prepared to leave through the front door, I suddenly found myself facing police officers with their guns drawn, yelling for me to get on the ground.

I complied and was handcuffed before being thrown into the yard with five or six of my friends who had come with me. Shortly thereafter, we were all placed in the back of a police car.

As the adrenaline began to wear off, I started to comprehend the severity of my situation. This was no mere after-school fight; it was far more serious than a typical middle school brawl or wrestlers sorting things out in the locker room. I realized I could be in serious trouble, and I had no idea how badly I had injured the other person at that party.

Eventually, I was taken to the local jail, where I was processed and placed in a jumpsuit. From there, they transferred me to the county jail due to the seriousness of my charges. We all stayed overnight there, and reality struck hard when I was separated from my friends. Since I was seventeen, they classified me as a youthful offender and put me in the section for those aged eighteen and under.

This all happened within about twenty-four hours.

Finally, my father came to bail me out. As I walked to his truck, I felt nothing but disappointment in myself and knew that I had let him down. It was particularly difficult for me because my dad had always been there for me. He and my mom had provided everything I needed to succeed: a loving family environment without any abuse. My issues seemed relatively small compared to those of many people I encountered in the county jail, yet I was creating my own problems.

When I got home and had that difficult conversation with my parents, the fear of disappointing them was overwhelming. It was hard to bear, but I also had to be careful not to be blinded by my arrogance and ego at that point in my life. Despite my mistakes, I still had a strong sense of self and a desire to test my limits. However, I did not know where to channel this energy. It was clear that my current path was not leading me to the life I truly wanted. Just like most seventeen-year-olds, I wasn't thinking much further ahead.

I went through the process of facing charges, though they weren't convictions. During this time, I still returned to high school to graduate. I was out on bail, and when I went back to school, the rumor mill began churning. One day, I was sitting in geography class when someone started a rumor that the guy involved in my case had died at the hospital, and I was anxiously waiting for the police department to arrive and arrest me for homicide.

I felt a lot of fear, and I remember going home and asking my mom if that was going to happen. She reassured me that, as far as she knew, it wasn't likely, but we were uncertain. That eased my fear a little.

Throughout that summer, I worked for my dad. I had been swinging a hammer and learning the trade since I turned thirteen. My dad had moved us to Oklahoma from Kansas when I was eight. He was an engineer by trade, but shortly after our move, he got laid off, which led him to become an entrepreneur.

He started his own concrete company, focusing on basement forming and building foundations. He became successful, driving his business forward while also working part-time as an engineer, which supplemented his income.

This was a time when I didn't know where my life was headed. My parents, Bible Belt Christians, wanted to impose more restrictions on me. They made it clear that they would only send me to college if I attended Oklahoma Christian Academy, emphasizing that I needed to go to a Christian college. They were very strict about my activities and kept a close eye on me. However, they were also careful not to push too hard, knowing that I might choose to move out, which would have been detrimental for me at the time.

I remember my dad inviting one of his friends from church over to talk to me. He thought that if I wouldn't listen to him, maybe I would listen to another man. However, I found the situation off-putting. One of my biggest struggles was with the religious community and how many people within the church seemed to cast shadows and shame on others. This left a lasting impact on my relationship with religion.

I felt an overwhelming sense of shame, not just in myself but also because the people around me acted as if they had never faced any problems or made mistakes. As I mentioned earlier, I wasn't a bad kid; I simply made a bad choice.

At that time, I was dating a girl, and her father, a successful construction worker who owned his own dirt work company, was a great mentor to me. I remember visiting their house one night when he said something that brought me a huge sigh of relief. All the people I was surrounded by, and those my parents wanted me to be around, made me feel like a bad kid doomed for failure, but he said, "You're not a bad kid. You just made a bad decision, and you need to fix it."

I thought, *Damn, he's right.* That summer, I worked for my dad, doing construction, swinging a hammer, forming concrete, and pulling rebar, just like I did every summer, earning minimum wage.

During that time, I was fortunate to work alongside an older gentleman who was closer to my dad's age and had known him for years. He gave me some of the best advice I ever received. He said, "Listen, son, you're in a tough spot. You've always wanted to join the military; you should consider the Marines."

Up until then, I had only thought about becoming an Army Ranger. I wanted adventure, to jump out of planes and push myself to the limits. This gentleman broke it down for me: "The Marines are different. Go apply and see what they say."

He advised me not to tell anyone, which was significant for me at that time. I had been following my parents' guidance on many decisions, and I trusted them; they were good people with a good life. I had doubts about my own thought process, and rightly so. However, when he said, "Don't tell anybody; go talk to them," it was a revelation. I realized that not everyone needs to know your plans. Sometimes, you just need to keep them to yourself and commit.

So, I did. One day after work, I went to the Marine Corps Recruiting Station and spoke with a recruiter named Staff Sergeant Chadwell. I felt lucky to meet him. As I explained where I was in life and my interest in joining the Marines, despite the massive amount of baggage I carried and my uncertainty about whether I could even qualify, he listened intently.

Then he said, "We can make it happen. Let's see what we can do."

Staff Sergeant Chadwell wasn't just another recruiter; he was a saint to me at that point. Why? Because I was far enough along in the court process that I was facing six months in a juvenile delinquency center, and they weren't going to ease up on that. They wanted to make an example out of me, and honestly, looking back at my age now, that was not wrong and was probably deserved. I did not want to go to juvie.

I knew the rabbit hole that awaited me there. I would likely get into fights, defend myself, probably catch more charges, and end up associating with the wrong crowd.

It's very easy for a young person to spiral down that bad path repeatedly. But joining the Marines was the right route for me. Staff Sergeant Chadwell had connections that could help. His father had been the chief of police in one of the areas we'd both grown up in.

Staff Sergeant Chadwell said, "I'm going to go to court with your attorney. I want to talk to him." Soon, they were working together. By that point, my parents were aware of my plans. I had already filled out all the forms and was in the processing stage. Now we just had to get through court.

My recruiter and my attorney went to court and explained, "Austin Hancock is going to join the Marine Corps. We believe this is the best option for him. If he enlists in the Marines, can he avoid going to juvie and instead join the military?"

There was a war going on in Iraq, and at that time, President George Bush was pushing for a considerable increase in troop numbers overseas. The military needed as many recruits as possible and was granting waivers to people with past troubles, including those caught with marijuana and other juvenile charges.

The judge agreed to our request, and I signed the necessary paperwork to proceed with my enlistment instead of going to a juvenile delinquency center.

Shortly after that, I completed the MEPS process, where I underwent my physical examination. Then I began the processing stage. In early 2006, I shipped off to Marine Corps boot camp, an experience that would change my life for the better.

CHAPTER 1: LESSON

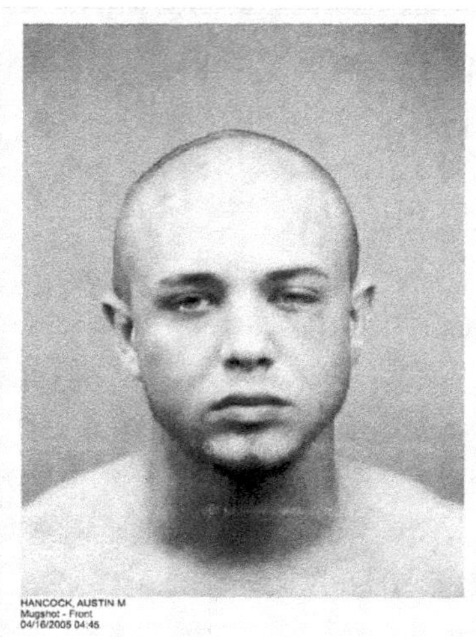

I am writing this book while sitting in a house worth over $4 million in San Diego, California, one of the most expensive counties in the United States. I drive the dream cars I've always wanted, from a Lamborghini to a Rolls-Royce. I have a beautiful family and have been happily married to my one-and-only spouse for twelve years.

I enjoy strong relationships with my friends and family, and I am fortunate enough to live where I want and how I want. The choices you make at a young age can have a lasting impact, but the decisions you make today can also lead to incredibly positive outcomes.

CHAPTER 2

I was eighteen years old, standing in Marine Corps boot camp, looking up at my drill instructor, a towering six-foot-five figure, who was yelling, "If he dies, he dies!" At that moment, I found myself questioning my decision to join the Marines, despite it being exactly where I wanted to be.

On Black Friday, when recruits receive their drill instructors, chaos and panic reign supreme. The goal of this initiation process is to transform us from civilians into Marines. My drill instructor was shouting those chilling words because one of the recruits on the third deck had attempted to commit suicide by jumping out of a window, landing headfirst.

My drill instructor, Staff Sergeant Gantt, had been overseeing our platoon on the bottom deck. We were moving our footlockers in and out, emptying them, filling them back up, and repeating the process. Meanwhile, every other platoon in our company was also experiencing the storm of chaos from their own drill instructors. This was all part of the initiation ritual on Black Friday, an effective way for the drill instructors to assert their authority.

As I carried my footlocker back inside, the recruit who jumped landed within ten feet of me. Staff Sergeant Gantt stopped us, looked down at the limp form of the recruit, and reminded us of the gravity of the situation, yelling, "If he dies, he dies." He knew we were to focus on our training rather than the incident unfolding before us.

After a while, they called for the corpsman and medical team. Thankfully, that recruit survived but was medically discharged from the military, exactly what he seemed to be seeking: a way out of boot camp.

That was my first day with our drill instructors, and in 2006, they were not just average trainers; most of them were combat veterans.

Some of my drill instructors had fought in Fallujah during fierce battles in Iraq from 2004 to 2005, and many had already deployed to Iraq and Afghanistan multiple times. Despite them being only twenty-five to thirty years old, they felt like gods to us. With their Purple Hearts and combat tattoos, they embodied the leadership I respected and needed.

Upon arriving at Marine Corps boot camp, I went through a week-long "receiving" process, which included medical checks and identification verification before meeting our drill instructors on Black Friday. All my instructors were combat veterans determined to prepare us for the reality of combat. They understood that we faced high risks, as we were joining the Marine Corps during a time of war, not peacetime.

Throughout boot camp, I learned essential skills, such as how to shave, march, walk, and address senior officers, transforming into a Marine. The boot camp experience lasts thirteen weeks, and I graduated with a meritorious promotion to private first class (PFC) after achieving the highest Physical Fitness Test (PFT) score in my platoon.

More than just military training, boot camp offered an opportunity to join a brotherhood and sisterhood. Being a Marine means holding yourself to a high standard, both during service and beyond, as emphasized by our drill instructors. Once you become a Marine, that identity stays with you for life.

Moving from a small town in Oklahoma to San Diego, California, was quite a culture shock for me. My time at the

Marine Corps Recruit Depot (MCRD) out west lasted just thirteen weeks, but I learned a lot during that brief period.

First, I discovered that you can push yourself much harder than you think you can. If you don't believe it, the drill instructors will certainly prove it to you.

Second, I realized that a lot of noise and chaos is just that: noise and chaos. You must learn to operate amid it because combat and the world outside are filled with the same challenges. You need to be able to make decisions even when everything around you is chaotic; your fellow Marines depend on you to get them and yourself home safely.

I no longer felt like a troubled kid. I had found a community, a brotherhood, a legacy. I felt as though I belonged to something larger than myself.

I was able to channel my energy, anger, ego, and testosterone into a unified purpose: protecting our country and, more importantly, protecting each other. I felt reborn. Prior to this, I had rarely ventured beyond Oklahoma. I had taken a few vacations, but moving to San Diego ignited a desire to explore. This came from a kid who was once afraid to spend the night at a friend's house in middle school.

This experience was exactly what I needed to reinvent myself and create a significant turning point in my life.

CHAPTER 2: LESSON

You can do more and push yourself harder than you think. Your mind will give up before your body. Don't stop.

Build the Foundation. Mind, Body, Soul.

AUSTIN'S FITNESS TRAININGS

Scan the QR Code to get your fitness in Marine Corps shape.

CHAPTER 3

After graduating from boot camp, I quickly headed off for ten days of "free liberty," which means I had time off. Every Marine Corps boot camp graduate receives ten days to return home, see their family, and enjoy a little rest and relaxation (R&R). After that, my orders were to report to my training school, where I would learn how to perform the job I had signed up for.

My job was in the infantry. Following my ten days off, I flew back to San Diego and began my training. At the School of Infantry (SOI), I underwent two months of training, covering everything from weapons handling to the realities of being a Marine. I learned how to shoot machine guns, fire rockets, throw grenades, and use rifles.

This environment was different from boot camp, where instructors constantly screamed at us. Now it was true training. The objective of the School of Infantry is to transform a Marine into a proficient operator in their weapon systems and job skills.

As an infantry Marine, my role was to learn how to operate these weapon systems and work effectively as part of a unit. We studied patrols and how the Marine Corps conducts itself in combat scenarios, ultimately gaining insight into what it's like to be at war.

After the two months of training, we graduated. One of the wisest decisions I made, which my parents insisted upon, was to serve as a reserve Marine. This meant I wouldn't go directly to a fleet unit; instead, I returned home and committed to one weekend a month and two weeks of training in the summer. As a reserve Marine, I had the flexibility to attend college or work, but whenever the Marine Corps called me up, I was expected to return for training.

However, in 2006, as I mentioned earlier, the war had commenced, and reserve duty became less abundant. Shortly after returning home from the School of Infantry, my battalion received orders that we were going to Iraq.

In 2007, I deployed to Iraq with my platoon, the very group I had trained with at my unit, building the camaraderie necessary to face combat together. Throughout our training, I learned in-depth about the combat theater we were entering and how to approach it.

I experienced firsthand the importance of leadership by connecting with my platoon sergeants and commanders, gaining insight into what constitutes good versus bad leadership. Even though I enlisted as a reservist, I was fully committed and living the life of an active Marine.

When we deployed to Haditha, Iraq, part of the Al Anbar province, we were aware of the challenges ahead. I still vividly remember my parents seeing me off in those last days before shipping out. My mother was crying, incredibly proud that I had chosen to become a Marine instead of going down a darker path. Yet, her fear was palpable, and my father later expressed the very real concern of whether I would return home or not

That fear resonated deeply with me as well. At just nineteen years old, I had signed my will, outlining what would happen to my nonexistent assets should anything happen to me. If I were to die, my parents would receive $400,000, a staggering amount to me at the time, but in hindsight, I know nothing could ever compensate for the loss of a child. I realized this was a feeling my parents had as well.

As my deployment approached, my mother insisted we have a serious conversation about what would happen if I were injured in combat. She raised tough questions about possibilities like losing my legs or other limbs, wanting to know how she and my father could prepare for such situations. I tried to lighten the mood with Marine humor, jokingly suggesting, "You can just give me go-go gadget legs. I'll be fine." It was a crude attempt to cope with the gravity of the situation, but I could tell my mom didn't find it amusing.

As I spent more time reflecting on my decisions, including signing the will and contemplating what lay ahead, I came to a profound realization: life can be very short. Combat brings you face-to-face with the stark realities of life and death. In those moments, everything you once thought was important fades away.

Materialism and the life I once knew, with my truck, my car, and all the things that seemed important to a nineteen-year-old, completely faded away when I prepared to step into a combat zone. In that moment, I realized that life can be short. This lesson would stick with me, guiding my pursuit of success in business and all my endeavors.

I understood that I had no time to waste, especially knowing that some of my brothers and sisters might not return home. I felt an obligation and a duty to live my life to the fullest and to be an example for those who didn't make it back. This sense of duty became ingrained in me the moment I signed my will.

In 2008, I deployed to Iraq. During my tour, I had some incredible experiences. I participated in multiple joint operations with special forces units, provided private security for battalion commanders, and worked security for VIPs, including Senator McCain, during the presidential elections. I even have a photo of myself shaking hands with Senator McCain on a soccer field when I was nineteen years old, holding a belt-fed machine gun in one hand and shaking his hand with the other.

These experiences were very real and opened my eyes to the world. It was no longer just about small-town life or casual training sessions with other Marines; it was about truly understanding the world and pushing myself to my limits. I feel very fortunate that in 2008, I returned home from this deployment alive, along with the rest of my platoon. I learned the value of life and gained a perspective on the world that is hard to put into words.

CHAPTER 3: LESSON

Life is short, and time passes quickly.

Make the most of the life you have, as some people's lives are cut short unexpectedly. We can never predict when our time will come or when we might experience a life-changing event, like a car accident or the last time we will say, "I love you," to our children.

So, prioritize what matters now and pursue the success that not only you deserve, but your loved ones deserve, too.

CHAPTER 4

After my deployment to Iraq, I was still in the Marine Corps but had limited time left in my service. I completed one more deployment to Morocco, Africa, as part of a joint operation with the Moroccan Army and other international forces. This deployment was non-combat, which was a relief for me. It gave me the opportunity to travel overseas again without the pressures of being in a combat zone.

I believe such experiences are crucial for many people returning from high-stress environments like combat. Mine allowed me to decompress and not feel as high-strung while in another country with my fellow Marines. I maintained communication with my brothers and engaged in operations that weren't life-threatening. In my view, staying connected and discussing our experiences with others who have gone through similar situations can help military veterans avoid PTSD.

Once I returned from the Morocco operation, I transitioned back to civilian life, which was difficult. It was challenging to adjust to a reality that no longer felt familiar. Having seen the world in a broader context, I found it hard to return to mundane tasks that I no longer found significant.

You could call me an adrenaline junkie or an action seeker; that was who I was before joining the Marines, and the military provided that thrill. After returning home and starting to work for my dad, I struggled to adapt. I was not the same person I had been before my service.

At twenty-two years old, I found myself moving back in with my parents, and all I could think about was breaking free and starting the next chapter of my life, accelerating forward.

I believe it's vital for military veterans, and for everyone in general, not to dwell on the past but to be excited about the future. However, I was losing that excitement and began to chase old vices and revisit problematic behaviors from my past. I felt very bored.

There's a quote from German philosopher Friedrich Nietzsche: "Under peaceful conditions, a warlike man sets upon himself." This was true for me at that time. I had developed a reputation as a heavy drinker during my time in the Marine Corps, which is part of the culture that we foster. Unfortunately, this was a negative aspect of my life that I continued to embrace after leaving the Marines.

I was still searching for adventure, and one of my coworkers suggested that we enroll in rodeo school to learn how to ride bulls. I was intrigued by the idea and signed up immediately. This example reflects a common trend: seeking something to fill the void.

The person who invited me to do this hesitated, waited, and ultimately didn't sign up. So, I decided to go alone, as I wanted to experience it either way.

So, I headed to Rose Hill, Kansas, to Sankey's Rodeo School, where I rode for the weekend. I felt a rush of adrenaline similar to what I had experienced in the Marine Corps. At this point in my life, I found myself constantly seeking adventure. I realized that my motivation for going was a sense of unfulfillment. I am still an adventure seeker today and look at life as an adventure.

I felt I wasn't reaching my full potential and lacked a clear mission. Back in the Marines, my mission had been straightforward: protect those around me and accomplish the tasks at hand every day. However, once I returned to civilian life, I became worried because I realized that despite working over ten hours a day in various jobs, operating equipment, doing dirt work, welding, and traveling around the Midwest, this was my life, and I saw no end in sight. There was no light at the end of the tunnel.

Fortunately, I had mentors early in my life. Even during this challenging phase, I could still go to the gym on weekends and sometimes during the weekdays. I would meet up with two of my older friends, who were ultimately like older brothers that I needed in my life.

Both of them were entrepreneurs. One owned a successful landscaping company, which he built from pushing a mower to managing a full-fledged business that allowed him to work as he pleased. To me, that was the ultimate lifestyle at that time. The other was a real estate investor, someone who'd had no knowledge of real estate when he'd started but had also been very successful. Neither had a college degree or a high school diploma; both jumped straight into work, hustling and creating their business from the ground up.

I learned a lot from these guys. Some lessons were spoken, while others were more implicit. One day, I was venting about my job: running equipment, pulling rebar, and working with concrete for my father. While my dad is an entrepreneur and a businessman, I was getting paid minimum wage, with limited opportunities to advance. I wasn't sure if my dad's approach was intentional or just part of who he was, but it turned out to be one of the best things that ever happened to me.

During a workout at the gym, as I was complaining about my life, one mentor asked me, "Why don't you start your own business?"

That thought had never crossed my mind. I said, "Well, how?"

I had all the objections, excuses, and reasons why it wouldn't work for me, yet he kept helping me, explaining, and answering my questions. He shared that, early in his career, he had gone bankrupt.

I thought that was horrible, and he told me he was able to bounce back quickly, within half the time. I just stared at him because, in the civilian world, one of the biggest fears people have is bankruptcy and failure, especially in entrepreneurship. I'll never forget when he asked me, "What are you scared of?"

"Failing," I replied.

He then asked, "What's the worst-case scenario? Really, play it out. What could happen?"

I thought for a moment and said, "I guess the worst-case scenario is having to move back in with my parents." At that point, I had already purchased a house using my savings from combat pay during my service in Iraq. I had no family and no expenses, so I'd managed to put money down on a property I owned, and I had a roommate who paid half the mortgage and worked for my dad as well.

My biggest fear was losing what I had achieved. Though my accomplishments felt insignificant to me, I still didn't want to lose them. I recalled that the fear in our minds can often be larger than what actually happens. I said again, "I guess I would have to move back in with my parents and feel like a failure."

He replied, "At least you tried, and you can get back up and do it again. Weren't you just in Iraq less than a couple of years ago? You could have died."

I agreed, but I pointed out that it was what I had signed up for. At that moment, I realized I had nothing to be scared of. I remembered being nineteen and signing my own will, understanding that life could be short. I had survived a war while many others had not made it home.

Not trying would be a disservice, not only to myself but also to the men and women who hadn't returned and to my future self. I knew I needed to take the risk of becoming an entrepreneur and start my own business.

At that time, I was still working for my dad. I wanted to start my business, but I was still very scared. I was attending college part-time to earn my municipal fire safety degree, as it aligned with my previous experience in a paramilitary organization. I began contemplating leaving the fire school to pursue my dreams.

I had envisioned a life where I worked only eleven days a month, lifted weights, ate well, and enjoyed a great lifestyle, escaping from construction forever. However, I was quickly shut down when I applied for the four or five openings at the Oklahoma City Fire Department. I found myself in a room with a thousand other candidates taking the written test. I wasn't the best test taker. Even though I scored between 85 and 90 percent on multiple attempts, the fact that there were only 4 open positions available and over 1000 applicants meant that I needed to score a minimum of 100 percent before I could even take the physical fitness test.

Unfortunately, I didn't even get the chance to demonstrate my physical abilities, which I had honed through military training and continued to maintain on my own. It was frustrating not to be considered for a position where I knew I could be an asset, simply because my written test scores weren't at the top. I realized that many of the applicants were also veterans, as a significant number of people were transitioning out of the military at that time, with the war in Iraq winding down.

I was competing for a job that paid around $35,000 a year and didn't offer much opportunity for advancement. Ultimately, I never secured a position with the fire department, despite earning my associate degree in municipal fire safety and completing EMT basic training and Firefighter I certification.

Looking back, I'm actually glad I didn't make it into the fire department.

CHAPTER 4: LESSON

Trust the process. Things work out for a reason, so continue to push hard and challenge yourself. Ask yourself, what's the worst thing that could happen? Write down your answer.

CHAPTER 5

I made $45,000 on my first custom home build, which was more money than I earned working for my dad the entire year.

How did I get there? I recognized the potential for change in my future and understood how money could be made without trading my time for it.

One of my mentors at the gym I worked out at encouraged me to start my own business. One day, I approached him and expressed my interest in making it happen. He offered me an opportunity: he would fund the first build if I did the work, and we could split the profits.

To me, this was a no-brainer. Here was someone willing to invest in me, and I was excited about it. The next day, I went to my dad's office to share the news.

I told him about the opportunity I had been given and my desire to pursue it. My father, being a wise and supportive man, wanted to ensure I was making the right decision. He counteroffered and said, "I'll let you keep 100 percent of the profit, and I'll help you through this process by co-signing on the lot. I may not know this person you plan to partner with, but I have connections in the industry that could be valuable."

This offer sounded even better to me. I could keep all the profit, and it was the same amount of work with added support. At that moment, I wasn't focused on the risks; the biggest risk in my life was not taking action.

So, I moved forward. I purchased a lot with my father's co-signature, which points to an important lesson: if you don't ask, you can't receive.

Every day, opportunities cross our paths that we might not see. The key is to get good at recognizing and capitalizing on these opportunities, especially at the beginning of your journey.

I completed the project in just under nine months. It was a ground-up, new construction of a nice house on an infill lot in an established neighborhood, which allowed me to anticipate the costs of nearby properties. I ensured that I was mindful of my profit margin.

I approached the build with care and aimed to do everything right. Ultimately, I successfully sold the property and walked away with $45,000 in net profit, 100 percent of which I kept.

I paid off the construction loan and purchased the lot, which allowed me to get my dad out of the co-signer role. At that point, I was officially in business and starting my first venture. I was fortunate to be able to work for him during this time, as it helped me cover my living expenses.

I would check on my project in the evenings and on weekends, and I was determined to see it through. I firmly believed that where there's a will, there's a way. I was hungry for more.

After cashing that first check, I became addicted to entrepreneurship and was filled with optimism. I continued, buying the next lot down the street and another lot in the neighborhood. There were only two lots left, and I was eager to make my mark.

After purchasing the second lot, I started building another house. However, it took a lot longer to sell than I had anticipated. During this time, I was paying interest on the loan, which was a tough but invaluable lesson. I learned that even if you make a profit, the process can come with challenges. A key takeaway is that anytime you make money and learn in the process, it's a win.

I kept pushing myself to grow. Ultimately, I made $25,000 on that project, but the experience taught me an important lesson: homes may not sell as quickly as you expect, and it's crucial to understand the market and your pricing.

I had no background in debt or banking; I came from a construction background. My sole focus was on being the best builder and managing the construction process without any financial education.

I was fortunate to have mentors who guided me throughout this journey; without their support, I could have made costly mistakes that would have set me back significantly.

I successfully secured the last lot in the neighborhood. I had custom plans ready for the house, designed by an architect and me. However, I was approached by someone interested in purchasing the lot. I explained that I had already put money into it and had a house plan I would sell along with the lot. I didn't know that this was a feasible option, but it turned out to be a valuable learning opportunity.

I decided to set my price. I projected that I could make around $25,000 to $45,000 on this new project, similar to my previous profits, so I included a $25,000 markup without having to do any of the work. I sold the lot for $25,000 more than I had purchased it for, along with the plans for that person to build their own home.

This person's father was a builder, and they wanted him to handle the construction. I recognized at this point that there was an opportunity to make money without having to oversee the entire process.

I initially overlooked the importance of financial education and lacked an understanding of debt and real estate, focusing only on construction. However, I persisted and expanded my efforts, ultimately taking on many more projects. From those initial projects, I gained experience with custom homes, worked on client houses with a cost-plus approach, and built a successful construction company that generated over $7 million annually before I decided to stop.

The entrepreneurial journey is filled with fears, doubts, and uncertainty. It's essential to embrace these feelings.

Every entrepreneur faces similar challenges, but we can't let them hold us back. This is how we learn and grow.

Think about learning to swim. We trust our swim instructors to keep us safe as we jump into the pool. Eventually, we learn to swim, a skill we carry with us for life. Similarly, when learning to ride a bike, a supportive parent might push you along until you fall and scrape your knee. You learn from that experience, get back on the bike, and soon, you're riding confidently.

Financial literacy and education follow the same principle, yet many people let their fears prevent them from taking that crucial leap. Don't let fear stop you; instead, use it to drive yourself forward.

CHAPTER 5: LESSON

Do not let fear paralyze you. Embrace it. Replace the word "fear" with "excitement."

CHAPTER 6

Life happens quickly. During this journey, I met the woman of my dreams and got married.

I had transformed my destructive behavior into positive actions, and it started paying off. I was focused on my business, with a wife who was pregnant and a one-year-old daughter. My daughters were born just thirteen months apart, so it was quite a ride.

I was living the dream and working hard, burning the candle at both ends to grow my business, all while taking on a second one. I wanted more. In my mind, more meant more, and I felt the need to expand.

I realized that if I was willing to endure the challenges I had faced in the Marine Corps, crawling through ditches, doing some of the dirtiest jobs, burning human waste in a combat zone, laying down fire, and risking my life, I had a strong work ethic. After coming back to the States, I had tackled gritty construction work, so I knew my work ethic would never be the problem.

The real challenge lay in where I directed my energy and how I applied that work ethic. So, I committed fully to building my construction company while simultaneously running a service business. Fresh into marriage and fatherhood, I was ready to do whatever it took to succeed.

I was on cloud nine, building my first house, 3,500 square feet, at just twenty-nine. I was moving into a gated community, into a home I had designed and that my crews had built. I was making money, feeling invincible, buying new SUVs, and trading them in for a new F-150 or F-250 each year to offset tax burdens as a builder and entrepreneur.

My wife had a small job but eventually quit. With her stepping back, the pressure fell on me to be the breadwinner, covering her income, health insurance, and the other benefits that came with her corporate job. She was betting on me, just as my kids were. I was betting on myself, convinced that I was invincible. I knew I was willing to work hard and do whatever it took to achieve success and growth.

However, not all businesses are created equal. Growing the custom home building company was far from easy.

Working with people involves managing their expectations, budgets, and realities compared to what actually happens in the field. It's not as glamorous as it may appear from the outside. You might see a new-construction builder living in his dream home, driving new vehicles, and showcasing his work on magazine covers at only twenty-nine years old, and think he has it made. But the stress was building up.

However, it wasn't my family's expectations that weighed heavily on me; it was the expectations of my clients. As a custom home builder working with high-end clients, CEOs, attorneys, and CFOs who were relying on me to create their dream homes, I quickly realized that their expectations were extremely high, while their understanding of the construction process was quite limited. Despite the significant income I was generating, I began to feel like my life was being drained away.

This wasn't why I had entered entrepreneurship or wanted to be a builder in the first place. I had become a builder simply because it was what I knew. Many of us find ourselves in careers or industries or starting companies based on what we currently know, rather than what we want to know or the kind of life we aspire to live. At the time, I didn't know any better and kept pushing forward.

I was determined to do whatever it took to succeed. By the age of thirty, I was one of the youngest members of the Central Oklahoma Home Builders Association, sitting alongside builders who were over sixty, people who had dedicated their entire lives to new construction and development. They became my mentors, and I got a glimpse of what my future could look like.

However, observing the stress they had accumulated over the years made me realize that I didn't want that kind of life. The life I envisioned for myself was one of geographical and financial freedom and the ability to live life on my own terms.

I had escaped the grueling ten-hour days in construction and the orders of life in the Marines, only to create a company that, while financially rewarding, had become more focused on customer service. This meant that it brought a significant amount of stress and unrealistic expectations from clients.

This experience taught me that not all businesses are the same. I saw a glimpse of my potential future while attending those board meetings with seasoned builders who had spent their lives in the industry. Many of them were still complaining, still stressed, and none were living out the dream life I aspired to achieve.

CHAPTER 6 LESSON:

Not all businesses are created equal. Think about your goals first. Create a business that provides you with the life you desire, rather than one you feel obligated to create right now.

Learn the necessary information to build the life you want and put that knowledge into action.

AUSTIN'S HABITS FOR SUCCESS

CHAPTER 7

While I wasn't living the financial dreams or experiencing the freedom I had always envisioned, I convinced myself that I just needed to put in the time to one day achieve those goals. I held on to the hope that if I worked hard enough, I would eventually live the life I desired.

Perhaps this mindset stemmed from my formal education or the belief that, one day, I would retire and experience financial and geographical freedom, the ability to do what I want, when I want, and where I want, as long as I put in the effort. However, I came to realize that this notion wasn't entirely true; life happens quickly, and I didn't want to spend my best years waiting until the end of it to enjoy myself. That wasn't the purpose of my journey into entrepreneurship.

As my business began to grow, focusing more on custom homes and taking on additional clients, my mindset was "more is more." I immersed myself in business, motivational, and self-development books, believing that to elevate my lifestyle tenfold, I would need to increase my workload significantly. I thought that to make more money, I needed to complete more deals, sell more houses, and take on more clients.

However, as anyone who has run a business knows, "more" doesn't always equate to "more." Higher gross revenue doesn't necessarily mean higher net revenue. In many cases, scaling a business can lead to increased stress levels, and as you grow, the margins you pocket often decrease. Being young, energetic, and ready to take on the world, with a beautiful wife and two daughters just thirteen months apart, I was eager to hit the accelerator and push full speed ahead.

I had the opportunity to become one of the builders featured in the Street of Dreams. This exclusive, invite-only event allowed select builders to construct high-end, custom homes in a unique development, with only eight others permitted to participate. Each home was a one-off, custom showpiece representing the quality and capabilities of their company. I saw this as a chance to elevate my building business significantly and increase my visibility through magazine features, news coverage, and various marketing strategies.

I viewed this project as an opportunity to grow my business tenfold, which involved taking on more debt. Building houses from the ground up requires signing loans in the hope that buyers will be drawn to these properties. Even though the homes were meticulously designed with my architect, designer, and team, showcasing top-tier appliances, tiles, and high-end automation, the financial burden of the debt was considerable.

I was astute enough to partner with another builder from the Oklahoma Builders Association for this project. My thinking was that we could split 50 percent of the profits from sales and also 50 percent of the risk involved. Several other builders warned me to be cautious when building such unique products; not everyone prefers custom designs. While you can attract clients by showcasing your capabilities during the month-long event, the risk of holding on to the property can be substantial. So, I forged a partnership for this house, secured a loan, and began the project.

Austin's tenfold method and more-is-more attitude filled me with high expectations and blind optimism about skipping off to make as much money as possible from my properties. I had a vision of baking in a net profit of over $250,000 on one particular property. To capitalize on that, I decided to secure another loan for a lot in a different part of the same neighborhood, one that wasn't included in the Street of Dreams. I believed that the attention from the show would drive enough traffic through the area, leading to significant interest in my property.

In line with my philosophy of "more is more," I took on another project in that neighborhood: a ground-up new construction that would match the caliber and size of the first house. On this one, I decided to go solo, taking all the risk but reaping all the reward, or so I thought.

If I planned to make $250,000 on the property I was partnered on, splitting that profit would mean I would only take home half of that. However, with the new property, I anticipated making a similar amount. Looking ahead to the end of the year, if everything went perfectly, though I knew it rarely did, I was aiming to net $350,000 to $400,000 from these two projects. I also hoped to attract more clients and scale my business, breaking the eight-figure mark.

The risk was substantial, as my only exit strategy involved building the houses and hoping buyers would come along, love them, and make offers. There were also holding costs to consider; I'd have to pay interest throughout the construction process and while the houses were on the market. Despite these risks, my optimism and excitement convinced me that the potential rewards outweighed the concerns.

At the same time, I was still managing projects that paid the bills, specifically custom houses for other clients on a cost-plus basis. My service business was thriving, and I was in the process of building a small team to help scale it. So, I thought, *What could go wrong?*

As we entered 2018, I was working on these two projects simultaneously. One was part of the Parade of Homes, an annual event where houses are showcased to highlight building capabilities and attract traffic. The other was featured in the exclusive Street of Dreams.

With this in mind, I brainstormed marketing strategies to boost my visibility. I envisioned people loving these homes so much that they would purchase them before construction was even complete, potentially bringing in a flood of new clients and elevating my company's revenue into eight figures.

However, not everything unfolded as planned. My blind optimism, combined with a hint of arrogance and my drive to tenfold everything, was ultimately based on ignorance. While the foundation of my plan was sound, it was riddled with shortcomings.

Throughout this time, I learned crucial lessons, sometimes painful ones, that guided me on my journey. One important lesson was that not all businesses are created equal.

We've discussed this before. Additionally, it's vital to understand that the lessons we face often serve a purpose: they steer us toward new opportunities. A mentor once told me that sometimes "the thing" leads you to "the thing," but you must be open-minded enough to recognize the new direction and know when to pivot.

As I navigated entrepreneurship, I struggled with failure, particularly due to my background in sports, like wrestling, where commitment was key. In my household, my parents enforced a rule: I could not quit any sport I started until the season ended. If, after that, I chose not to continue with that sport, they were fine with it. However, quitting mid-season was not an option.

I firmly believe in this principle, and I apply it in my household today. While this mindset can be beneficial, it can also be detrimental, especially when you're determined to succeed. In entrepreneurship, it's not just about staying committed; it's about knowing when to pivot and seize new opportunities that could lead you to the life you truly desire.

The two houses I was building sat on the market longer than I had anticipated. I was hemorrhaging money, paying $5,000 a month in interest for each one. At that time, I had built my own custom home, 3,500 square feet in a gated neighborhood with a beautiful yard and all the custom amenities. I was now thirty years old, with a young family consisting of two daughters under three years old and a wife who had just quit her job. What could possibly go wrong?

I pressed on, making those payments, but as I scrutinized the numbers, I eventually realized that my financial situation was deteriorating. I struggled to pay bills through my company. As the projects concluded and the market shifted, I desperately hoped that someone would buy one of those houses. Unfortunately, they did not sell nearly fast enough for my liking.

My service business was barely scraping by, and while I was working on various custom projects for clients, the profits were swiftly consumed by the interest payments, maintenance, water bills, utilities, and other expenses associated with the two houses on my and my partner's balance sheets. Each of these projects was valued at over a million dollars.

If you're unfamiliar with the term, a "spec house" is a speculative investment, which I learned later on. It's a hope that you can sell these properties for a profit. If you don't, you lose. The market, along with appraisals, dictates the property's worth. Ultimately, you must have the stomach to carry these loans without knowing when someone will come along to buy the homes.

At that time, I didn't realize how stressful it would become. As my money went out the door, the stress only increased. I was open about my challenges, perhaps to a fault, at the young age of thirty. I would share my stresses and strains with my wife, which, in turn, added more pressure to our home life. I later discovered how stressed she truly was.

She never expressed this during the process; instead, she gritted her teeth and endured it while raising our children and trying to keep our costs down. I assumed she was managing just fine. After the storm passed, I realized that she had been extremely stressed and didn't know how to cope. She had internalized it.

I'm an external thinker, often venting my thoughts, which only amplified the stress in our personal lives and our business. At that point, I knew I had to make a decision.

I would wake up in the middle of the night and struggle to get any rest, barely managing two or three hours of sleep. It wasn't because the babies kept me awake; it was the constant dread of potential bankruptcy or failure, which terrified me.

I didn't want to fail. People had just started to see me as an entrepreneur, and on the outside, I looked successful, with expensive cars and a new house. I had it all, the whole nine yards.

I distinctly remember why I decided to work so hard and grow my company. It was during the time we were moving into our custom 3,500-square-foot home. As we settled in, bringing our personal belongings into this house, I looked around the neighborhood.

I was familiar with the area, having spent the last eight months building the house and visiting the job site almost every day throughout construction. However, I had never fully considered my neighbors. Most of them were in their fifties and sixties, doing well for themselves and in retirement mode. However, instead of feeling inspired by this, I thought, *This is it?...*

I recall a conversation I had with a friend over coffee. He said, "Man, I'm so proud of you. This is awesome! Do you think this is your forever home?"

I couldn't believe he thought I would settle down in one place forever. I thought, *This is it. I'm thirty years old, and this is all I feel I can do. It's as if I'm just settling down, ready to quit and throw in the towel, waiting to simply defend what I have left for the remaining years of my life.*

But that's not me, and that's not how my story was going to end.

This feeling was part of why I decided to go all in, pushing harder and try to accelerate my journey as an entrepreneur. More is more, right? Not necessarily.

As I managed two properties, the debt piled up, and credit cards became a constant burden. My service business wasn't performing well enough to meet our financial needs, and we found ourselves spending more than we were making across the board. We had to stretch our credit cards to pay our employees first and ensure we could eat while also managing personal debts.

It was then that I realized I needed to put my own house on the market. If I could sell it, I would accumulate around six figures, giving me some breathing room, if not a lot of profit. Then, at least, I'd have the space to make decisions and continue pursuing entrepreneurship.

During those sleepless nights, I started waking up and exercising on the treadmill in my garage. I used that time for fasted cardio, trying to keep my body and mind in the best possible shape to handle the weight of responsibility and the tough decisions I had to face.

I told myself, *You're the man of the house, Austin. You made these decisions. You have to fix this. You need to figure it out.* But I didn't know where to turn for help.

Fortunately, I came across a book called *Extreme Ownership by* Jocko Willink. I listened to the audiobook during my treadmill sessions, and one lesson struck me deeply: if you are the problem, then you are also the solution. This concept of extreme ownership resonated with me.

In the construction industry, blaming others is all too common. Contractors blame each other for mistakes. I blamed subcontractors for not showing up on time, and I told clients about all the issues we faced. It created a perpetual cycle of blame, a very negative, toxic environment that I had grown up in, but I was blind to its detrimental effects on my mindset.

I realized that if I blamed the market, the subcontractors, the banks, and interest rates, then I had no control over anything. I couldn't focus on the actions that would actually drive positive change. This realization clicked for me.

As a former Marine, I needed to reassess my thinking: if I was the problem and the one who got us into this situation, then I could also be the solution. This understanding led me to take the step of putting my personal house on the market, even while the two other properties were draining our cash flow.

By a stroke of luck, our house received significant interest and sold a few months later for around $600,000, helping to ease our financial burdens.

We secured a contract for one of our properties, and it sold, which relieved us. We ended up making a little over $100,000, but that wasn't all profit. Most of that money needed to go toward paying off the credit cards we had been stretching, helping us get out of debt, and, ultimately, funding the two houses I had built and was still making payments on. The situation felt never-ending because we didn't know when someone would come along to buy those projects.

In true builder fashion, I moved into one of my spec houses, the one I had built on my own, not with my partner. This allowed me to avoid adding more expenses while living in a house I had already built. Renting would have been a higher expense than what I was already paying, so I decided to keep that house on the market while we lived in it.

My wife understood the situation and was prepared to leave at any moment. Unfortunately, I didn't fully grasp how much this was wearing on her at the time. As a young mom trying to settle in with our children, she sought stability. However, she also knew that we had committed to this plan.

We discussed it and were willing to do whatever it took. This was a pivotal moment in my life, when I realized that if I was committed to doing whatever it took, I would embrace a strong work ethic.

No one could stop me. I was willing to work night and day to solve problems, whether I was making pennies as a Marine or getting paid hourly as a contractor. Ultimately, that hard work needed to pay off.

This led me to think about what else could help me achieve the lifestyle I truly wanted. I questioned why I was sacrificing my entire life for the hope that everything would pay off someday, allowing me to become the version of myself I desired, to be both geographically and financially free. I had convinced myself that one day, after a certain point, like retirement, or when specific conditions were met, I would finally be fulfilled. Yet, I lacked a solid plan.

As I faced the discomfort of ongoing financial strain, combined with my newfound understanding of extreme ownership, I began to seek solutions. The essence of extreme ownership is to find solutions to the problems you created. Even if you didn't create the problem, you can still search for a solution.

We moved into the house that was on the market and lived there for nine months before we eventually sold it. Fortunately, during that period, the other property I had with my partner sold as well.

Here's another lesson I learned: sometimes, you have to pay to resolve problems. We had the Street of Dreams house on the market for almost a year before finally receiving our first offer, and it was for less than what we had invested in the property. This meant we would essentially be paying to sell this house.

My partner, who had been building for thirty years, told me that, sometimes, you have to pay to move on because the uncertainty of not knowing when the next buyer will come along can be worse. You start hoping that someone will buy it for at least the purchase price or higher, just to cover the debts you've accumulated.

We faced a decision: we could either accept the current offer and pay $65,000 at the closing table to sell it, or we could wait for a potential buyer with no clear timeline in sight and no end to the pain of the monthly payments. We both agreed it was time to sell. Fortunately, I had sold my primary residence and made a little over $100,000 profit.

I was able to use half of the $65,000 I needed from that capital to move this other project forward and eliminate the ongoing expenses that were weighing heavily on me, my family, and my business. So, we went ahead and wrote a check for $65,000 at the closing table for the sale of the Street of Dreams project, and I split the loss with my partner.

I still remember that day vividly. When we wrote that $65,000 check, our real estate agent, who was representing us in the sale, walked away with a $45,000 commission based on our pre-negotiated agreement. This was a valuable lesson for me. The agent did everything right; they took photos, brought their team to market the house, and did their job effectively. However, they took absolutely no risk. Their only risk was the possibility that we could fall out of contract and they wouldn't sell the property, which would mean no commission for them.

Unlike us, they didn't have a million dollars of debt tied up in the property. They didn't build it from the ground up or deal with the struggles of coordinating subcontractors. They didn't go through the process of furnishing and designing the home or fixing issues along the way. All they did was market the house, and in the end, they walked away with a $45,000 check, while my partner and I had to write that $65,000 check.

Example

Sale Price: $1,000,000
Closing Costs & Agent Fees: $65,000
Loan Balance (Debt): $1,000,000
*The house sold for **exactly what I owed on it.***
*After paying the loan, there was **no money left** to cover the fees.*
*So, I had to **bring cash to the closing**.*
Money I Paid at Closing: $65,000

The lesson I learned was that not all businesses are created equal, and taking on debt, especially bad debt, is never a good idea, particularly when you have only one exit strategy. I realized that I needed to understand the other side of investing, such as listing properties, to hedge my bets and stop losing money while making profits. This risk prompted me to ask myself, *What else can I do?*

During my self-development journey, I became genuinely invested in learning. I continued to read, listen to podcasts, and do whatever it took to grow my knowledge.

I distinctly remember telling my dad during this time that I wanted to learn more and that I was interested in real estate investing. I sought his advice because he had successfully owned a construction company for many years. I also asked other builders in the room at our board of directors meeting if they knew anything about real estate investing. Unfortunately, everyone gave me the same answer: no, they did not. They were experts in building and construction, not real estate.

Since I needed this information, I decided to do my own due diligence. I read books on real estate investing, listened to relevant podcasts, and researched online, whatever I could find. I was eager for change, and I knew that my work ethic would help me achieve my goals as long as I was in the right financial vehicle.

You can work very hard in the wrong business and still never reach your desired destination. I believe that many entrepreneurs, and people in general, sell themselves on the idea that they will "make it one day" without any actual plan or data to support the outcome they hope for. Not all businesses provide freedom, whether geographical or financial. Most can tie you down. In my service business, I dealt with employees, trucks, insurance, and meeting clients on location. In my building business, I constantly hoped for clients and the successful sale of houses we constructed.

I had a lot of hopes but no guarantees. I wanted to operate my business based on numbers. After learning and reading books about investments, I realized that successful investors approached things differently.

They didn't focus on designing the perfect home or using the latest, trendiest finishes. Instead, they concentrated on the numbers and real data. That's when it hit me: this is how businesses should be run.

At this point, I faced a decision: should I continue to be a builder and keep pushing in this direction, or was it time to pivot? Though I didn't say it out loud, I knew in my heart that I needed to pivot, but I wasn't sure where to find the education I needed. How does one learn new information? Most of us grow up connecting with people in our market, family, and friend groups.

Keep in mind, this was before YouTube became popular and social media could provide educational resources. The information I received came from family, friends, or people I perceived as successful, like those at church or the gym, which is what got me into entrepreneurship in the first place. Unfortunately, I didn't have anyone in my circle who was knowledgeable about real estate investing or who had the time to teach me.

I realized that I had to invest in my own education. Despite still dreaming of the glamorous life of a custom home builder, complete with accolades, magazine features, and awards for homes I had built, I recognized that none of that mattered. It wouldn't lead me to the life I truly wanted.

I needed to find what would give me that. As I immersed myself in real estate investing education, I distinctly remember seeing some investors walking around in flip-flops and T-shirts. They didn't have to wear blazers or cater to clients, and they didn't need to maintain a certain persona to attract business. After all, working with custom clients meant hoping that they would choose me to build their home.

These investors were living their lives as they pleased, traveling and doing what they wanted, because they ran their businesses based on numbers. They made smart deals that made financial sense, and they had multiple strategies to ensure their success. Ultimately, they were able to truly enjoy their lives. They designed their businesses around the lifestyle they wanted, rather than shaping their lives around the businesses, which is what most people tend to do.

At this point, I also realized I had my own internal struggles and personal challenges. Growing up in Oklahoma, the Bible Belt, I had always aspired to live on the West Coast. I was obsessed with the car culture I had adored back in high school: the tattoos, watching Jesse James on TV, and shows like *Motorcycle Mania* and *Monster Garage*. I wanted to embrace that lifestyle, but I just didn't know how to achieve it.

After leaving the Marine Corps, I was completely covered in tattoos, with two full-sleeve tattoos by the age of twenty. I never thought that this would affect me mentally in my thirties as a business owner, but it impacted me significantly because I felt I was leading two separate lives. I couldn't be the investor who dressed as he wished, sported tattoos if he chose, lived wherever he wanted, and traveled when he pleased.

Instead, I had to be Austin Hancock, the builder who wore collared shirts and concealed his tattoos, assuming that potential clients would not hire me because of them. Ultimately, this meant living an internal battle for self-identity.

This situation was frustrating and difficult; I felt like I was sacrificing my authentic self for the hope of one day being who I truly wanted to be. My morals and ethics never changed, but my perception of myself and how I believed others perceived me held me back from becoming the person I was meant to be.

These insecurities crept in and haunted me in various ways. Coupled with the stress of projects that wouldn't sell, they led me to invest in myself and finally take the leap into real estate investing. Even before I made that jump, we were still facing significant financial pressure.

Before the spec house we were living in was sold. I decided to invest a substantial amount of money into my own growth because I recognized I had no other way out. I was determined to escape this so-called rat race that I had just learned about and truly become an investor. Despite feeling cornered both mentally and financially, this turned out to be one of the best decisions I ever made. I realized at that point that I needed to learn new information, apply it, ask questions, and repeat that process to change my situation.

CHAPTER 7 LESSON:

Sometimes, the lessons we need to learn aren't the most comfortable. I believe that times of struggle and strain guide you toward a better future, but you have to be willing to listen. Reframe your mind to say, *This is a test I have been given and need to pass in order to achieve my goals.*

When your back is against the wall, you must commit to changing who you are, as this will ultimately determine where you go in life.

CHAPTER 8

With my back against the wall, I knew I had to make a decision. In the Marine Corps, there's a phrase we often use in combat: "Move or die."

To me, this means you can't stay in one spot. It signified life and death during my time in the Marine Corps, especially in the infantry and in combat. If you don't move, the enemy will locate your position, attack you, flank you, or kill you. You're constantly moving toward the enemy, toward the objective, or toward extraction or insertion.

Momentum is key. Recognizing this, I understood I had to make a serious decision. My wife and I faced this together, despite the stress she was enduring and the massive uncertainty we were experiencing. We decided to invest $52,000 in a two-year real estate education program. This was before the era of online education. We had to fly out to a specific location once a quarter for masterminds, sitting in a formal classroom with PowerPoints alongside other real estate investors and aspiring investors.

We networked, educated ourselves, and put ourselves in an uncomfortable position that we knew was necessary. I kept reminding myself to get comfortable being uncomfortable. At that point, I was fortunate to have paid down some credit card debt, which allowed me to accumulate more debt, because I didn't have the cash.

It still felt like the right decision because I was willing to put in the work; I just needed new information to apply. I was determined to do whatever it took, whether staying up late or digging trenches, to achieve success. With new information at my disposal, how could I possibly fail?

Fortunately, my instincts were correct. I charged $52,000 on two separate company credit cards because I didn't have sufficient credit limits on one. Eventually, we had to sell some of our belongings to manage the process. Luckily, during the time we carried this debt on our credit cards, we managed to sell the projects I mentioned in the last chapter, accumulating six figures. We used that money to pay down the credit cards and move into a rental house, which was both humbling and necessary.

Sometimes, you have to take a step back, reassess, and make a strategic choice so you can take five steps forward. That was my situation. We attended classes and seminars where we learned about fixing and flipping properties, buy-and-hold strategies, creative financing, mobile home parks, multifamily units, and commercial real estate.

I became hooked. It was incredible, networking in these rooms, exchanging contact information with others, and learning from high-level investors doing hundreds of millions of dollars in deals.

I was captivated and wanted to apply what I was learning. I distinctly remember that over the past couple of years, I had accumulated a few rental properties, but they had become the bane of my existence because I didn't know what I was doing. My arrogance had gotten in the way; as a "macho man" and a builder, I saw $700 a month in rent as a waste of my time, even though I owned these properties. I thought, *Why should I worry about that $700 a month when I am receiving six-figure checks weekly from clients for custom home projects?*

It's important to note that when I collected those six-figure checks, a significant portion went toward materials, labor, insurance, and other expenses. The profit margins in construction are not as large as many people perceive. But my attitude was still a barrier for me. Attending those events was humbling.

I clearly remember one of the successful instructors at the seminar asking me what I did for a living. I told him, my guard still up, about how I was a prominent builder and how successful I was at a young age. He then referred to me as a speculative investor. I hadn't encountered that term before. I said, "Spec? Isn't that just for spec houses?" I didn't even know what the full term meant.

He explained that speculative investing means you're banking on one person buying that property. All of your time, energy, and investment are dependent on that one property, or those multiple properties, selling on the market. I added, "Well, I also do custom homes," and he acknowledged that.

He said, "So, you left a job to work for someone else, earning a lot more, but ultimately, you're still in customer service."

At that moment, I realized that while I had quit a stable job to earn more money, I was doing ten times the work, which didn't feel rewarding. It was a valuable lesson.

That single lesson was worth the $52,000 investment in the program, as it opened my eyes to what I was doing wrong. However, that wasn't all I learned. I also discovered creative strategies for selling properties in one of the classes during my second visit to the program.

I took that knowledge home and immediately applied it to two of my rental properties. Remember, I was a builder who previously didn't care much about these properties and was a rather neglectful landlord. But when I implemented the creative exit strategies I had learned during the second seminar, I was able to turn around those properties and make $25,000. Rather than losing money due to my previous arrogance, I turned that situation into a profitable one.

I realized that investing in myself was an infinite return. The knowledge I gained was something I wouldn't forget, and I would continue to build on this education, applying it across all areas of my financial and personal life. I became addicted to self-development and then to learning about real estate investing. I saw it as a financial vehicle that could provide active income through wholesaling, fixing and flipping, or creating loans, as well as passive income by holding rental properties and loans. Ultimately, this would set me up for long-term success.

In my mind, there was no better business than this. I could earn significant active income ($200,000, $300,000, even half a million dollars) while simultaneously building wealth and accumulating assets. This strategy would help me reduce taxes and grow my portfolio, which I could eventually pass on to my children, if they chose.

I was hooked. I continued to learn, educate myself, network, and make connections. The $52,000 I invested quickly paid itself back, and I applied what I learned diligently. My wife attended these meetings with me, traveling to various locations.

Before the rise of social media and technologies like Loom or Zoom, if you wanted to learn, you had to book a flight and attend classes in person. This traditional approach allowed us to network, collect contact information, and build new friendships, forging an invaluable network that would help us make millions and improve both our personal and business lives.

As we pushed forward, I saw opportunities on the horizon. However, halting a company I had built wasn't feasible, especially with ongoing projects and obligations to current clients. I knew I had to keep moving forward.

Challenges arose. In 2020, during the COVID-19 pandemic, building material prices skyrocketed, labor was scarce, and many people had more money than they had ever seen and were eager to make decisions after being cooped up at home. I had numerous clients wanting to take on more projects, and I felt foolish for not seizing those opportunities to grow the construction company I had always envisioned.

But in the back of my mind, I knew I didn't want to build forever. My goal was to make as much money as possible, finish the projects at hand, and eventually transition into real estate investing. Even though I had invested considerable money in real estate and was seeing a return, I was only actively involved about 15 percent of the time. My wife was learning the information and leading our real estate investments while I continued running our service business and taking on new-build clients to ensure we could put food on the table and pay off our educational debt.

Despite the challenges, I managed to keep going. However, with clients eager to build their dream homes in 2020, shortages in materials meant I couldn't provide accurate estimates on lumber costs, delivery dates for materials, or availability of essential appliances. I had never encountered a time when I had so many clients willing to spend money on building custom homes, yet the bottlenecks were material shortages, labor issues, and delays in finishing projects.

The situation went from being merely stressful to extremely stressful. Clients often claim they understand the process when they sign the contract and express excitement about building their home, but in reality, their expectations are much higher than what can actually be delivered. They believe they understand, but they often do not grasp the full picture.

At this point, I took on numerous projects, allowing me to scale my business and increase profits, which helped me overcome the debts I had accumulated. I was highly successful in making a lot of money throughout 2020 and 2021 from these projects, but it was also the most stressed out I had ever been. This experience taught me that I needed to trust my instincts and pivot toward real estate investing.

Inspired by the success of others, I started to apply what we were learning in our mastermind group. I realized I needed to unwind my building company and commit to the next step: real estate investing. So, I finished the projects I had started throughout 2020 and 2021, no matter how challenging or stressful they were.

In retrospect, it was one of the best decisions I ever made, and I'll always remember it. My wife, on the real estate investing side, was doing deals here and there. She eventually got her real estate license and began listing properties for other people while also engaging in retail-style transactions. It's important to note that obtaining a real estate license isn't necessary to be an investor, but it can serve as a valuable tool for making more money.

I will never forget a project she completed where she bought a property, turned it around, and sold it in less than thirty days, making a $25,000 profit. This amazed me because I was busy working on projects for others, and I distinctly remember doing a small project for some friends of ours. Working for friends can be particularly challenging. This specific project was a $400,000 addition to a house.

I ended up being tied to this project for an extended period, carrying the warranty for over a year. When I looked at the potential profit from this project and broke it down by month, I realized that my wife had made significantly more money in thirty days than I would earn from that project. That realization was eye-opening.

I did not take on any more clients after experiencing that profound realization. When God, fate, or alignment presents you with clear signs, such as the numbers guiding your path, it's essential to listen and remain coachable.

You must align yourself with your true goals, and that's exactly what we did. I finished my last project in 2021 and simultaneously began building my real estate business. The years 2021 and 2022 were ideal for establishing a real estate company because the market was on the rise. Property appreciation was soaring, and there was a significant demand from both hedge funds and retail clients, resulting in price wars and bidding wars.

I found myself more captivated by flipping, buying, accumulating, and wholesaling affordable housing than constructing unique, custom-designed houses with a team of designers and architects. The financial returns were substantial and came quickly. The assets I acquired were tangible and devoid of emotional ties.

We fully committed to this new venture. After I completed my last custom build, we managed to acquire up to thirty rental properties a year, adding them to our portfolio, and were successful in flipping between thirty and forty houses annually, generating profits ranging from $10,000 to $80,000 per project. We simultaneously built a large portfolio of seller finance deals where we became the bank and held the loans on houses instead of renting them out. This was a strategy we learned from our education and still highly use today.

I built a team and dedicated myself entirely to this new path, investing resources even when we lacked them. Looking back, it was the best decision I ever made. We also ventured into wholesaling to acquire our own properties, generating between $60,000 and $100,000 a month in wholesale revenue alone, on top of our existing activities.

To say we were busy would be an understatement, but we were genuinely excited. This work freed us from the stress of dealing with end clients and customer service challenges. I completed the custom home I had scheduled for 2021 and never looked back; I was all in.

We purchased a 3,300-square-foot office space, remodeled it, and began to build an entire team and business in the way I had always envisioned.

CHAPTER 8 LESSON:

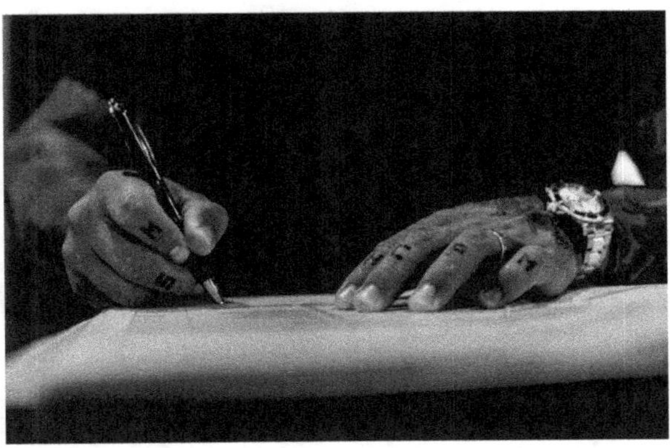

Don't be afraid to pivot. Sometimes, one opportunity leads you to another. Quitting in business only truly occurs when you stop pursuing your goals.

Keep your focus on your ultimate objective. The pathway to get there may vary; what matters most is that you build your business around the life you desire.

CHAPTER 9

Real estate investing was supposed to provide me with financial freedom, geographical freedom, and the lifestyle I desired. However, I found myself stressed out with the demands of my business. I wondered, *How did I end up here?*

I started in real estate to grow a successful business and enjoy a fulfilling lifestyle. Yet, I suddenly felt trapped, as if I had built another cage for myself. After establishing my office and my team, I was still hungry for more.

Despite achieving impressive sales numbers and generating substantial income, I clung to a "more is more" mindset. I was applying this perspective to real estate investing without realizing that I was merely creating a different version of the same trap. My team included cold callers and a boiler room with our team of salespeople, agents, and transaction coordinators.

We were expanding into a 3,300-square-foot office that featured a conference room and a podcast room, and everything on paper looked fantastic. Revenue was flowing in, projects were progressing, and we had a project manager to oversee them. However, I lost sight of my original goal in real estate.

One crucial lesson I learned from my mentors was that the only money that truly matters is the net profit, the money you actually keep after expenses. Many people boast about their gross revenue, but no one likes to talk about making $10 million a year while spending $11 million. That's not a position anyone wants to be in, but the big numbers definitely sound appealing.

I began to recognize that our marketing budget was ballooning. We were spending between $20,000 and $40,000 a month on it, while our top-line revenue from wholesale remained stagnant at $100,000 a month. This realization pushed me to analyze my business through a lens focused on the numbers.

Examining our overhead costs, including employee salaries and commissions, made it evident that we were headed down a precarious path. Meanwhile, I was increasingly stressed because my work ethic compelled me to arrive earlier than anyone else. As the owner and boss of the company, I felt that a true leader leads from the front.

While building my company and remodeling our office, I was simultaneously constructing my final custom home in Oklahoma. As a builder, it made perfect sense for me to take down a house on an existing property and rebuild to create immediate equity upon completion. After we stabilized and rented out our previous home, selling the ones that caused us headaches and stress, we found ourselves living in a rental property.

This rental was quite nice, complete with a neighborhood pool, located in a gated neighborhood, and, importantly, very affordable for the Midwest. At $1,800 a month, it was a significant improvement compared to the over $10,000 monthly payments we were bleeding on interest for the previous two houses. We had applied the knowledge gained from our real estate education to our situation effectively.

I clearly remember the moment I realized this approach could truly work. After living in the rental for less than a year, the landlord informed us that he intended to sell the property and would not be renewing our lease.

At that point, we were already in the process of building our own custom home. We had shifted our focus entirely from taking on client projects to building for ourselves while also expanding our real estate investing business.

My mindset was simple: more is more. I was ready to tackle challenges head-on, much like the Kool-Aid Man bursting through a wall. So, I proposed to the landlord, "Why don't we buy the house from you?" At the time, I didn't have the money upfront. He wanted $350,000, but I was confident that with my newly acquired real estate knowledge, I could make the deal work.

Understanding that knowledge paired with experience is crucial for real estate transactions, I felt well-equipped. I offered him $300,000, explaining that he wouldn't have to pay any realtor commissions or closing costs, as we would cover those expenses. He wouldn't need to fix anything, list the home, or wait for it to sell. We could simply buy it directly from him. He agreed, and it turned out to be one of the best decisions he ever made.

Fortunately, my wife was already a real estate agent, and we had a clear plan for what we would do once our custom home was complete. Just three months later, our new house was finished. We purchased the property we had been renting for $1,800 a month using private capital. I approached one of my investors and said, "I want to buy my primary residence, and I plan to sell it once my custom home is completed. Will you fund this deal?"

"Absolutely," he said, "for X amount." I paid him a small interest payment for the time that I held his capital and purchased the property with cash, eliminating monthly payments and further reducing my overhead while we built our custom home.

Once our house was completed and we were ready to move, we listed the rental property we had just bought for $395,000. The market had improved slightly, and we had made some cosmetic upgrades worth about $5,000. We sold the property in less than thirty days, pocketing roughly $90,000, which helped us recover all the money we had spent on rent, expenses, utilities, and other costs.

This real estate investing approach works, and the more knowledge and experience you gain, the more successful it becomes. I was hooked. We moved into our custom home, which was within walking distance of the newly remodeled office where we had set up our team. However, this also brought back stress.

Why? Because we had multiple employees, significant overhead, and a big marketing budget. I had inadvertently created a corporate lifestyle for myself. I found myself showing up before everyone else and leaving after them, even though my goal was to build a lifestyle business.

My intention was to work from my laptop or cell phone and have the freedom to be where I wanted, when I wanted, and how I wanted, while still engaging in real estate transactions without being tied to a specific location. However, this was impossible with this model. I had in-person staff and multiple salary obligations, which made it challenging.

As interest rates increased, our marketing expenses continued to rise, leading to a decline in our profit margins. Consequently, I was compelled to let some employees go, not only to create the lifestyle business I desired but also to avoid putting ourselves in a financial pinch again. Learning from past experiences, I recognized it was time to shed unnecessary weight, and we did so.

By downsizing and realizing we could hire people virtually to maintain the same performance, we began to align with our original goal: to live freely and design our lives. At that moment, I had an epiphany: I needed to work backwards. I needed to learn how to design my life first and then build the business around that vision.

Before this, I only knew that I wanted to do more and build my business. It took me multiple attempts and experiences across different ventures to realize fully that I needed to work backward. I hope this provides some context and shows you that you can reverse engineer the process.

What does your dream life look like? How do you want to live? How do you want to present yourself? How do you want to walk and talk? What do you want to do, and what steps will get you there?

Once you start eliminating distractions and recognize that only a few financial vehicles can truly help you achieve your dreams, you'll begin to see how you can design those financial paths. This awareness will have the most significant impact on how you live. You'll realize what you shouldn't be doing and focus on the few essential actions that will drive you forward.

At this point in my journey, while visiting various projects, checking on them, and building my business, I decided to venture into social media. I created accounts on Instagram and YouTube and wanted to share more of myself with the world. I enjoyed connecting with people and loved growing my business, branding myself, educating others, and showcasing our work.

I was fortunate to connect with many other veterans through social media. I'll never forget attending a real estate convention in Dallas, where I reached out to a friend I had met online, Taylor Cavanaugh. He was a former Navy SEAL and French Foreign Legionnaire, and we quickly bonded over our military backgrounds and shared attitudes.

Taylor was flying in from France after leaving the French Foreign Legion to do a podcast in Dallas at the same time I was attending the convention. We decided to meet at the hotel, and I suggested we record a podcast together. We did, and our discussion was enlightening, which brought us even closer as friends.

I remember asking him, "You're getting out of the French Foreign Legion. You must have a lot of belongings after living there for almost five years. What are you bringing back from France?"

Since he was originally from Southern California, I expected him to have a Connex box or a lot of items to move. At that time, my mindset was still tied to the substantial possessions I owned: a 5,000-square-foot custom-designed house I had just built, a 3,300-square-foot office nearby, the artwork I had selected for my office, my cars, and my gym. I enjoyed all of these things, but they were potentially holding me back.

I didn't realize this until Taylor replied to my question. He said, "No, bro. All I've got is two seabags." That brought back memories of my time in the military, which I had completely forgotten.

I had completely overlooked the fact that all I'd had were a couple of sea bags to my name. Taylor said something I'll never forget: "Freedom of movement is the most important thing to me." That statement resonated deeply with me, especially as someone who felt obligated to be present all the time in my company to motivate and lead others. This created a cycle of business that, while I had no problem with leadership, made me feel like I was building a prison for myself.

I wanted to design my life and truly live it. When Taylor mentioned "freedom of movement," it struck a chord with me, and I could tell my wife, who was with me, felt the same way. We exchanged looks that conveyed we were both thinking the same thing.

I'll never forget what it was like to move from one house to another. At that point, we had already lived in four or five houses, and our kids, still under the ages of five and six, had moved just as many times in their short lives. Throughout those moves, we had cleansed ourselves of things; we'd thrown items away, donated them to charities, or given them to friends. We didn't carry everything from house to house.

We were on the brink of freedom of movement, but hadn't fully realized it until Taylor explained it so simply. It's not about material possessions; it's about freedom. Sometimes, possessions can hold you back. There's nothing wrong with accumulating experiences or enjoying things like cars, houses, or watches, but it's essential to remember that from ashes to ashes, dust to dust, we will all eventually be gone. The house you call yours will one day belong to someone else. The clothes you wear, the shoes on your feet, even the cars you drive, will end up as trash or in someone else's hands.

I had learned this through my experience of buying real estate from a purely numerical perspective, yet I had never applied that mindset to my personal life. I invested so much time and energy into designing custom homes for myself, thinking about garage sizes, bathroom dimensions, hallways, and ceiling heights with great detail. However, tastes and decisions change over time.

So, I came to realize that I shouldn't be married to the idea of a "forever home." Possessions are just things. What matters more is learning to be mobile, agile, and versatile.

Freedom of movement. That's what I truly wanted.

CHAPTER 9 LESSON:

THE MOBILE · AGILE · LETHAL FRAMEWORK

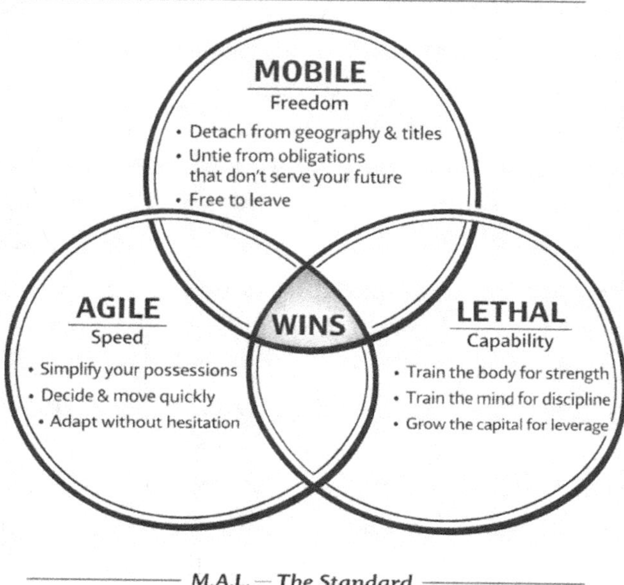

Mobile, agile, lethal. I created this framework, and I teach it at my in-person events.

"Mobile" refers to the ability to move when, how, and where you want.

"Agile" relates to how quickly you can react to situations. How light on your feet are you? Are you tied to a geographical location because of your children's sports or your mother-in-law? Are you allowing minor obstacles in life to hold you back from pursuing your dreams, or is it really just fear?

"Lethal" emphasizes the importance of being able to protect my family. I practice jiu-jitsu, maintain my strength through weight training, and continually sharpen the skills I developed as a Marine.

But consider this: How lethal are you from a financial perspective? How well do you understand your finances? Can you provide for your family the way you want to?

I like to think of finances in this way: When you're on an airplane, they instruct you to put your own oxygen mask on first in case of an emergency. If you don't do this and instead place your child's mask on first, you risk passing out and becoming unable to help anyone.

This same concept applies to your life. Stop telling others what they should do unless you're living the life you desire. Focus on helping yourself first so you can genuinely lead and assist others.

That's what it means to become lethal.

CHAPTER 10

After adopting the mobile, agile, lethal mindset and simplifying the company, I stopped walking to my office and even ceased driving to the office that was within walking distance. The large office that I had designed, remodeled, and built ultimately became vacant, with no employees.

I let the majority of the team go, and those we still needed worked virtually, which was freeing and one of the best feelings I had ever experienced. The business was still performing well; we were profitable, and I began to realize that we were living a life of our design, creating some of the freedom of movement that I had learned from my good buddy Taylor.

We became addicted to this lifestyle and started to expand our mindset and thought processes around it. Throughout this journey, I never attached my happiness to material possessions. I was always happy, whether as a Marine grunting through the trenches or swinging a hammer in construction.

It's essential to recognize the difference between happiness and satisfaction. I was content, but I wasn't satisfied, and that's okay. It's all right to be hungry for more. Just remember that you create your own happiness regardless of where you are.

Moving into our dream home, which we built from the ground up, was an amazing experience. It was a three-story, 5,000-square-foot house with a full gym in the basement, a pool, a hot tub, and all the amenities, including a media room and a private suite. It also had a four-car garage to accommodate all my toys and belongings.

However, after conversing with my buddy Taylor and reflecting on our journey of unwinding the business to become more mobile, agile, and effective in our lives and work, I realized that this might not be what my wife and I truly wanted. I remember asking her whether building another house across town would make a difference in our lives. She looked at me and said, "No, absolutely not."

We enjoyed our current neighborhood, but we loved change. We liked to switch things up. The excitement of moving, doing something new, growing, and progressing was what truly mattered. When you're on the path of progress, that's when you feel the most successful. That was where we were, and we were addicted to it, as we should have been.

We began contemplating the idea of selling our home and thinking about where we would like to live. We considered some of the top locations, asking ourselves, "If it were up to us, given the opportunity we've created through our increasingly virtual real estate business, where would we choose to move?"

Not many people get the chance to relocate based solely on their preferences. Most have to move due to job commitments or family obligations, such as helping a sick relative. Very few get to choose their ideal environment, and this opportunity was a direct result of the hard work, education, and personal development we had invested in ourselves throughout our entrepreneurial journey.

We looked at places like Boca Raton and Fort Lauderdale in Florida, as well as Scottsdale in Arizona. Ultimately, though, San Diego, California, still tugged at my heartstrings. My love for San Diego stemmed from my time in the Marine Corps and the vibrant energy of Southern California. I had long been captivated by the SoCal culture, even before I'd gotten married. My wife was surprisingly open-minded about all our options. Given how many times we had moved and the experiences we had gone through, people often thought we were crazy.

"Why would you stop building?" they would ask. They didn't understand the challenges we faced, nor did they know what our version of success looked like. We felt like outcasts, outsiders who took risks. Then, they saw us find success in real estate investing and thought, *Wow, he did it again.* They didn't know about the troubles and trials we had endured, but that was okay; if they hadn't experienced similar struggles, they wouldn't understand.

So, what was next? Momentum. I often talk about the importance of momentum and carrying it forward. When given an opportunity, seize it. At that point, we decided to lease our office space and put our house on the market. Knowing we lived in a highly sought-after neighborhood, we were confident it would sell quickly.

Before listing it publicly, my wife suggested that we text our neighbors to inform them we were selling our home and give them an opportunity to have one of their friends move in. This was a niche neighborhood within an older development, and we had built the newest and largest house in the area. This approach would allow someone else to buy our property without a real estate agent, ultimately saving us a commission fee and streamlining the process.

She texted the friend group from the neighborhood, and within two days, we had the property under contract for $1.3 million, with a cash offer, ready to close within thirty days and no inspections required. We were blown away. This was the perfect outcome.

If there was a sign from God or a higher power, this was it. We would be foolish not to take this opportunity. But where would we go?

We didn't know, but we knew we had to act. We quickly signed the agreement and began the process of selling our home, which would finally close in roughly thirty days. We were a little stressed about our office, which we no longer used; it was completely remodeled, but still had a monthly payment we didn't want to carry.

However, as fate would have it, within a week of signing the contract on the house, the office was leased for five years. We would earn $2,000 a month in profit from this lease. It felt like a strong sign we should move forward. Was it scary? Yes. Was it exciting? Yes. Was it what we wanted? Absolutely.

I quickly booked tickets to San Diego because I wanted to convince my wife to move there before we considered any other location. My heart was set on San Diego. I had been transformed there; my experience in the Marine Corps had reshaped me, and I felt a powerful pull back to the beaches, the weather, and the energy that filled me there.

We took the trip, looked at houses, and devised a plan, but we found nothing. Moving to a new area and trying to absorb everything in just one weekend was not enough time to get us geographically oriented. This made my wife nervous.

Keep in mind, she graduated with just 40 people from a small town in rural Oklahoma. This move would be one of the biggest transitions she had ever made, while I had traveled extensively during my time in the Marine Corps and was eager to embrace the change. Still, she was committed and ready to take the leap.

Since we didn't find anything to buy, we decided to explore leasing a property at first. Leasing would give us the flexibility and freedom to move without being tied to a mortgage, especially in a location that was still unfamiliar to us.

So, we planned our exit: our office was leased, our house was under contract, and life was beginning to feel exciting. Life is short, and we decided it was time to make this move.

CHAPTER 10 LESSON:

The path will illuminate as you walk it. Don't expect to have all the answers in advance; instead, take each step forward, and clarity will come.

Trust in God, the higher power, and yourself. As long as you are aligned with these principles, you will prevail.

CHAPTER 11

My wife and I were excited. We felt as if we were truly living the life we wanted, in line with our purpose. We felt successful because we were living authentically. However, this sense of fulfillment didn't align with what everyone else expected of us.

When you share your big dreams with people who have a limited mindset, they often respond by telling you why it won't work or projecting their insecurities, disguised as advice. This is a crucial lesson in entrepreneurship and life: people often speak from their own fears and insecurities, but they present them as facts.

Many couldn't understand why we chose to move to California, thinking we were absolutely crazy. "Isn't it expensive there? Aren't there crazy people? Aren't there homeless people?" Their doubts instilled a bit of fear in us, but we knew we had to block out the noise.

I quickly connected with a friend from social media, Randall Parks, who was a real estate agent and a fellow Marine. Having the brotherhood of Marines made it easier to connect, even with those I hadn't known during my service. Randall told me, *"San Diego's like a bubble. People just don't know. The perception you see on the news is often skewed; it's amazing here, bro. Definitely come!"*

Despite the noise from family and their uncertainties, we pressed forward. It was essential to trust ourselves, trust the vision, and walk the path as it unfolded. We had been given this vision for a reason and didn't want to squander it.

Each of us has a vision, often rooted in childhood dreams. While many things change over time and societal programming tries to dictate what is logical or financially sound, it's the wild ones, the outsiders, who don't adhere to those expectations, who carve their own paths and push past the noise.

I still remember the dreams I had when I was ten and the people I admired. Although much has changed since then, the essence of who I wanted to become remains. Ultimately, it's about embracing the life you aspire to live and the character you wish to embody.

Think of your life like a movie. Design it as though you are the main character. Who is that character? How does that character walk? How does that character talk?

As we discussed in the previous chapter, it's essential to design your life the way you want it. You must also shape the person who can achieve, sustain, and lead that life. Everything connects.

Self-development is a crucial tool, and surrounding yourself with others who are on a similar journey is key to success. So, we decided to pack up and move to San Diego, leaving behind our friends and family, except for a few friends I had met through social media who agreed to support us. Our family, especially my parents, continued to support us from afar. While they were sad to see their grandchildren go, they were excited for our future and eager to watch us grow.

We weren't fully prepared, but we knew it was something we wanted to pursue. Selling our house in Oklahoma and making over half a million dollars in cash from the equity we had built was an amazing jumpstart for our success in a more expensive area. The rent we faced in San Diego was triple the mortgage we had in Oklahoma, but I wasn't scared. Why? Because I felt a strong calling toward this new life and trusted the process.

Building a real estate investing business virtually, with employees across the United States and around the world, allowed me to buy and sell property from anywhere. I became geographically free, operating from a laptop and a cell phone while creating teams and establishing local connections through networking.

I knew we had the tools to continue this journey, and nothing would change whether I was doing deals in my kitchen in Oklahoma or in San Diego. We had built the foundation that would provide the life we wanted, one that offered us geographical freedom and the ability to live where and how we wanted.

The work was on us, and we committed to showing up every single day. I recognized that when people would raise concerns about the costs of living in California compared to Oklahoma, it's all relative. If you are an entrepreneur or a business owner, consider this:

Having a fixed income can make the cost of living a significant issue, while being an entrepreneur allows your income to depend on your work ethic, network, connections, and location. In San Diego, you are statistically more likely to connect with people who have a higher net worth than in Oklahoma.

For simple math, consider that there are approximately 3.8 million people in San Diego County and about four million in Oklahoma. Statistically, the likelihood of encountering wealthier individuals is higher in San Diego. If it costs more to live here, it's because there are people making more money. And if others can succeed, so can I, and so can you.

There are more job opportunities, more companies, and an improved lifestyle; it's all possible. Shortly after moving to San Diego, we continued making deals, and I'll never forget that within three months, we refinanced part of our portfolio, which included 26 single-family homes, all from our kitchen table in San Diego. The proof was undeniable.

We were experiencing a new reality. Real estate investing can serve as a pathway to escape your current life or to create the one you truly desire. It is achievable, and we were demonstrating this through the use of mobile notaries and the convenience of Zoom calls and mobile technology.

Increasingly, people seek geographic freedom and value it more than holding onto a family home that belonged to their grandparents or parents. People's priorities are shifting from the traditional white picket fence and the American dream to a desire to explore and live a life that they design for themselves. You can be one of them.

You just need to remember these less ons.

CHAPTER 11 LESSON:

Freedom of Movement with Real Estate Investing

You can build a portfolio remotely and maintain mobility. Live wherever you want while conducting deals across the United States. To succeed, you need to learn the ropes, understand the process, educate yourself, take action, and then repeat these steps. Today's world has freed us from geographical restrictions.

Instead of making excuses, focus on creating the life and business you desire.

CHAPTER 12

Sunny San Diego is my home, and I'm focused on building a life of my design. Social media played a significant role in my journey as I worked on my brand and put myself out there. I remembered how I learned about real estate investing and how to start my first business from my mentors. While some people criticize gurus and self-help groups like those led by Tony Robbins, the truth is that these figures have transformed more lives than traditional education ever could. I guarantee that they changed my life.

Before I found those mentors, I didn't have a place to learn about real estate investing. There's no formal setting where you can acquire these skills or connect with others who are living the life you aspire to have. Being able to ask questions and apply the answers to your own life is crucial.

I started to educate others on social media about how to get into real estate investing, and I was thrilled to see people succeed, complete deals, and build a network and community that benefited both me and others financially. More importantly, I wanted to show them how they could live their best lives by implementing the lessons learned from previous mistakes.

Networking and connecting with people through social media, podcasts, and even workouts became something I truly enjoyed. As an extrovert, I loved learning from others and sharing knowledge. This was how I originally put myself out there and absorbed valuable lessons from my experiences.

As my real estate portfolio continued to grow, Alysha, my wife, took control of most of it, managing it from a distance. I felt a deep desire to help and educate others on how they could achieve similar success. The influx of inquiries I received when I first started in real estate was overwhelming. However, I wasn't sure how to assist them effectively. I would offer sporadic advice to friends over dinner, attempting to explain the ins and outs of real estate, but I quickly realized that people often don't value free advice.

Have you ever invested your time to help someone and provided them with all the tools and guidance, perhaps met them at the gym or did whatever it took to support them, and they still didn't implement any of it? I was baffled. It appeared that many didn't grasp the importance of taking action.

Did they not want it as much as I did? I was confused until one person reached out and asked, "How much would you charge to teach me how to become a real estate investor? How can you help me achieve what you have accomplished in your life through real estate?"

I didn't know what to charge initially, but I came up with a proposal. I was surprised to receive payment from someone eager to learn, though it wasn't what I had paid for my education. They were serious about it.

Their commitment led to success, and I realized that when people invest in themselves and their knowledge, they take the process much more seriously than if the education were free. Reflecting on my experiences, I've noticed that every time I invested in masterminds, real estate groups, courses, and education, I was far more committed than I would have been if I had received the information for free.

I was thrilled to witness my students making progress. One of my first students earned $29,000 within the first eighty-one days of working with me because he took action. He was determined to change his life and committed to doing so. That was all it took.

I advised him to take on more projects and set up a backup plan, an exit strategy from his job. He was a smart young man, an engineer in the oil and gas industry, making decent money and living in a trailer for three weeks a month for his job. Recently married, he saw a bleak future ahead and hated it.

When he embraced the idea of becoming a real estate investor, took control of his finances, and decided to quit his job, he saw his dream come to fruition. Now, as a professional real estate investor, he continues to grow his portfolio, having accumulated more than three properties while flipping multiple homes and earning over $50,000. He transformed his life in a short period, proving that, sometimes, all we need is one piece of information or one win to change our lives completely. One conversation can make a significant impact.

I can recall several pivotal moments when I had enlightening conversations with mentors, both paid and free, that shaped my journey and brought me to where I am today. While my wife focused on building our real estate portfolio, I managed refinancing, buying, flipping, contract for deeds, and seller financing, all while shaping our portfolio to fit our lives.

One common confusion in real estate investing is the sheer number of ways to make money in this field. When I started teaching others, I broke things down into a simple process to help them understand and take action because I remembered how it felt at the beginning: *What should I do next?* It's easy to feel overwhelmed, like you're drinking from a fire hose and can't catch your breath. That's why we broke things down the way we did.

As a result, people began to enjoy the process. The brand, the business, and the mentorship grew into a massive community, helping hundreds of people achieve their version of success. I pushed myself to the next level and decided to host an in-person event.

I was nervous about speaking in public. Even though I can easily carry on a conversation in a group, the idea of speaking in front of people was still intimidating. But then I remembered: I wasn't scared; I was excited. It's all about reframing your thoughts and pushing forward.

Move or die. I hosted my first event in San Diego at my home, and it was a huge success. There were tons of people, and we had a great time. I met my community in person, worked with them, and experienced the fulfillment of seeing others win, not just online or through phone calls, Zoom calls, or educational courses, but face-to-face.

I witnessed their transformations and heard how excited they were for the future. It was the most rewarding experience I've ever had.

One important topic we discussed was the ability to create your own schedule. Most people don't have the opportunity to control their time, which means someone else is controlling it for them. Escaping what is often called the rat race can be very challenging at the start. However, once you begin a side hustle, like real estate investing, which requires minimal time, you can start to regain control of your time. This is the catalyst for designing your own life.

One of the biggest components of my success is maintaining my fitness. I follow a regimented routine that I learned from the Marines: waking up early, working on my self-development, and understanding what truly moves the needle in my business.

Too often, small business owners or individuals focus on many tasks that don't yield the outcomes they desire. They get caught up in busywork rather than what really matters.

They often micromanage their work to avoid the most challenging aspects of running a business: having tough conversations, negotiating deals, communicating with lenders, growing the business, driving revenue, analyzing finances, and focusing on the metrics that truly matter. When I first started as a builder, I would frequently visit the job site to avoid looking at the financial records. I didn't want to confront what we were earning or spending.

It felt uncomfortable. I've never liked numbers or math.

In school, I struggled with these subjects, and I convinced myself that I wasn't capable of handling them. However, the reality was that understanding the financial side of my business was crucial. Instead, I spent my time engaging in tasks that felt easy because they were familiar to me.

Remember to get comfortable with being uncomfortable. This principle applies to your business. Just because you don't enjoy certain tasks, it doesn't mean they shouldn't be done.

Sometimes, it's critical to focus on the areas that have the most significant impact, such as finances, metrics, leadership, and roles like CFO or CEO. Concentrating on sales, driving revenue, acquiring more properties as a real estate investor, or securing better financing are the essential activities that truly move the needle.

Have those conversations. Pick up the phone and take action. It's the most important thing you can do.

CHAPTER 12 LESSON:

Don't Fall Victim
to Analysis Paralysis

Avoid being paralyzed by overthinking, fear, or dwelling on negative thoughts. Trust the process, gather the necessary information, and take action.

This is the only way we truly learn. Commit to the journey and overcome obstacles. The most important aspect of this process is who you become along the way. By developing into the person capable of sustaining the life you desire, you will ultimately achieve your goals.

CONCLUSION

If I can do it, you can, too. There are people out there who are less intelligent, less dedicated, and less committed than you, yet they are making more money and living their dream lives simply because they refuse to let fear hold them back. They take bold actions without overthinking.

You will face setbacks, and that's perfectly okay. Just remember, it's only truly over if you give up.

Information is useless if it isn't applied. Many people continue to consume information, watching YouTube videos, listening to podcasts, reading books, or enjoying audiobooks, without ever taking real action. They never fully commit.

Their focus is too broad, preventing them from achieving success in any one area. If there's anything that I can do to convince you that real estate investing can bring you the success you desire, it is this: it is not a get-rich-quick scheme, but it is a guarantee for wealth with commitment.

So, commit, take action, follow the process, and don't be afraid to make mistakes. Get back up and tackle life head-on. Remember, when you are aligned with your purpose and making progress, that's when you truly feel alive.

THANK YOU FOR READING MY BOOK!

If you are ready to take the next steps, want guidance to avoid mistakes, are committed, and are serious about living your life by design, scan the QR code below, and let's have a conversation.

I appreciate your interest in my book and value your feedback, as it helps me improve future versions.
I would appreciate it if you could leave your invaluable review on Amazon.com with your feedback.

Thank you!